The Museum of London

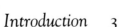

Designed and produced by
Thames and Hudson Ltd, London

Gallery plan by Brian Elkins

The Museum of London
London Wall
London EC2Y 5HN
Tel. 01-600 3699

Printed and bound in Japan by Dai Nippon

The Museum Departments

The Museum's main departments are arranged chronologically and deal with Roman, Medieval, Tudor and Stuart, and Modern London. In addition, there are departments of Paintings, Prints and Drawings, and Costume and Textiles. There are two archaeological field and research units – the Department of Urban Archaeology and the Greater London Archaeology Department – which are responsible for excavation within the City of London and Greater London respectively.

The Education Department provides programmes and activities for individuals and organized parties of all ages and abilities.

A research library, which specializes in London history, is open by appointment only.

Many of the objects reproduced and described will be found on display in the Museum's permanent galleries, while others serve to illustrate the rich collections on which the Museum can draw when devising temporary exhibitions.

The Roman architectural collections in the Guildhall Museum
1884; from the *Illustrated London News*
The stonework and the mosaic were excavated from Bucklersbury (where the Temple of Mithras was later discovered) in 1872, and were displayed in the east aisle of the new Guildhall Museum which opened in 1876. The mosaic and the figure of a soldier on the left are in the Roman gallery of the present Museum.

Introduction

London is the oldest, largest and most cosmopolitan city in Britain. Founded in about AD 50, it has 6,765,100 inhabitants, speaking 134 languages. It covers an area of 1,580 square kilometres, divided into 33 separate boroughs. It has been the capital of England since the Middle Ages, of Britain since 1707, and until recently was the hub of the largest empire the world has seen.

The size of the city, the wealth of its architecture and artefacts and the richness of the records relating to its history tend to deter most people from doing more than selecting one facet of London's present or past for further study. Nevertheless, the need to form an overall picture of the place has generated a whole series of books from the sixteenth century to the present day. The rise in educational standards at the beginning of this century, for example, provided a ready public for encyclopaedic books picking up all the scraps of information about places and customs in London. At a more serious level there has been no shortage of attempts to bring together the various strands of London's history. There is, however, only one museum that attempts the task: the Museum of London.

But how can a city of such immense diversity be portrayed within four walls? The answer is that it cannot – at least not fully. However, it is possible to pick out the main features of the development of London and the life of its inhabitants. To do this the Museum must build as complete a record of London as possible in the form of objects, pictures and other sources of information. Although, as the following pages show, you will see many works of art and craftsmanship of the highest quality from all periods, they are here primarily because they provide evidence of significant aspects of London's history. As a result you will find in the Museum almost every conceivable sort of object. There are stone axes, Roman sculptures, medieval toys, a dead chicken, prison cells, Chelsea porcelain, a painting by Sickert, fittings from a barber's shop, a bust of Lilian Baylis and an incendiary bomb. They are not displayed in galleries of archaeology, ceramics, paintings or costume, but linked together by period and topic, so that you can begin to glimpse what it was like to have worked as a clerk in Edwardian London, or to understand why London Bridge is where it is.

Layout of the Museum

The Museum of London was opened in December 1976 by Her Majesty The Queen. A splendid new building was designed by Powell, Moya and Partners as part of the City of London Corporation's plans for the redevelopment of the western end of the street known as London Wall. Except for the hall of the Ironmongers' Company, which the Museum now encircles, the site had been laid waste by bombing in the Second World War.

The new building has four parts. The bronze tower which rises above the main structure contains commercial offices and belongs to the Corporation of London; it has nothing to do with the Museum. The other three parts form the Museum, which is entered from the upper-level walkway. There is a main court surrounded by two floors of exhibition galleries, a wing containing the lecture theatre/cinema and education rooms, and a rotunda with restaurant and garden. These elements are linked by the entrance hall and covered external concourse.

The Surrounding Area

The Museum's site is a historic one. To the east it is immediately adjacent to the wall of London, the earliest surviving evidence of corporate activity by its citizens. This stretch of the wall was first constructed in the third century, and takes in part of the defences of a military base established by the Roman administration about a century earlier. The new defence remained in service, with regular repairs, until the sixteenth century. Traces of

Sign of the Bull and Mouth Inn
Probably late 18th century; from the Bull and Mouth Inn, St Martin's le Grand; wood and plaster; 1370 × 1900mm

all these periods of the wall's history can be seen both from the Museum galleries and in the garden adjoining the Museum.

On the west side of the Museum is Aldersgate Street. Along this route, from the Middle Ages to the early nineteenth century, the coaches left for York, Newcastle and Edinburgh. The 'departure lounges' were in the Bull and Mouth Inn, which until it was demolished in 1831 stood south-west of the Museum at the corner of St Martin's le Grand and Angel Street; its sign is in the Museum. To the north of the Museum is the Barbican Centre for Arts and Conferences.

The Barbican area grew into a suburb of the City in the early Middle Ages, around the church of St Giles Cripplegate (visible from the Museum's medieval gallery) which was founded in 1090. The name 'Barbican' is first mentioned in 1348 as a street running on the line of the present Beech Street tunnel, and originated from a medieval semi-fortified house in the area, belonging to the Suffolk family.

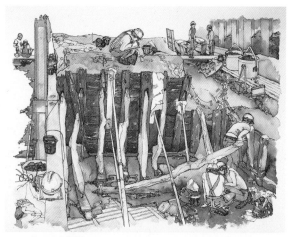

The Billingsgate excavation
1982; watercolour by Sharon Pallent; 422 × 535mm
One of a series of watercolours and drawings commissioned by the Museum as part of the process of recording London as it is now. In this instance, it is the Museum's own activity as the principal field archaeological unit for London that is under scrutiny. The excavation produced evidence of quays on the river from the Roman period to the present day, and traces of St Botolph's church.

Fennings Wharf, 1984
Staff of the Department of Greater London Archaeology remove samples, for tree-ring dating, from the elm piles forming a protective 'starling' around the piers of the 12th-century London Bridge.

(Below) **The defences of London, adjoining the Museum**
The visible remains are of medieval and later date. The bastions are 13th century; the wall in the background is 18th century or later, on earlier foundations. The centre of the original Roman fort lay to the right. In the background are the church of St Giles, Cripplegate, and the Barbican Centre.

Piccadilly Circus, c. 1952
Since this photograph was taken, there have been several proposals for the redevelopment of the area, none of which has been realized. Now that agreement has been reached, Eros is being moved, and most of the advertising has gone.

(Right) Hansom cab, c. 1900
'A hansom cab . . . has been presented by Mr and Mrs David MacAlister to the London Museum at Kensington Palace. It is difficult to realise that with the present rate of progress in mechanical traction this will be one of the few specimens of a vehicle which was always, to a very great extent, peculiar to London.' (The Autocar, 8 June, 1912.)

(Left) Central London, looking west from the National Westminster Bank tower in the City
London's position was dictated by the construction of a bridge across the Thames by the Roman authorities in about AD 50. This linked the two areas now known as the City and Southwark, both settled in Roman times. A third focus developed in the 11th century on Thorney Island, a raised tract of land adjacent to the river and surrounded by water, where Westminster Abbey and the Royal Palace of Westminster grew up. Since that time London has always been twin cities: Westminster, the seat of Government, and the City, the centre of commerce.

(Left) **London Museum displays in the ballroom of Lancaster House**
The cases display costume and other items of the 17th and early 18th centuries. The rider of the horse is wearing a buff coat of the mid 17th century.

(Right) **Sir Guy Laking setting out to lead the remains of the Roman ship to Kensington Palace, 1912**
The remains of a Roman ship were discovered in the construction of County Hall. Attempts were made to preserve the vessel, and it was displayed at the London Museum until the Second World War. When it came to move the vessel to the present Museum it was found that most of it was in fact modern plaster.

Later, in the eighteenth and nineteenth centuries, the Barbican area came to form part of a crescent of industrial activity related mainly to the printing and clothing trades which extended into Little Britain and Smithfield. There were a number of religious meeting houses, and the memorial outside the Museum entrance commemorates John Wesley's conversion in 1738 at one such house in Nettleton Court, on the site of which the Museum now stands.

History of the Museum

The Museum of London resulted from the amalgamation of two separate museums: the Guildhall Museum in the City and the London Museum in Kensington Palace. The Guildhall Museum was the older of the two institutions. It was established by the Corporation of London early in 1826 as a 'place for the reception of such antiquities relating to the City of London and the suburbs as may be procured or presented to this Corporation'. Its first gift was a fragment of Roman mosaic from Tower Street in the City. It was not until 1837 that the collection was first referred to as a

museum and three years later it was given a special room in Guildhall. The Corporation's initiative antedated by almost twenty years the foundation of museums by other municipal authorities. It was also unusual for institutions of the time in that it did not seek to establish itself as a miniature British Museum. Instead it concentrated on antiquities dug up in the City, objects connected with the Corporation and a selection of other items from the City such as inn-signs and trade tokens. It was not without rivals. Charles Roach-Smith, a pharmacist in Lothbury, and later in Liverpool Street, formed a private collection of antiquities which he had recovered from excavations in the City. In 1840 he opened his Museum of London Antiquities, which he sold to the British Museum in 1854. A hundred and twenty years later it was necessary to make replicas of one or two pieces of Roach-Smith's collection in the British Museum in order to complete our present displays.

The first Guildhall Museum was not a very dynamic institution – more a private collection than public museum. In 1855 Charles Read, a member of the Court of Common Council (the local authority for the City of London), sought

support for a free Public Library and Museum. It was necessary, he said, if only because the British Museum was so inaccessible to the public, being open on Mondays, Wednesdays and Fridays only. Read was unsuccessful, but eventually in 1872 work was begun on a new Guildhall Library and Museum. The building still stands adjacent to Guildhall in Basinghall Street, although it is no longer used for its original purpose. The Museum remained in these premises until the outbreak of the Second World War. Considering its size, it was fairly popular: in 1910 it was visited by 153,242 people, compared to 630,882 visitors to the British Museum. But thereafter it had a rival, the London Museum, first in Kensington Palace and later at Lancaster House.

The London Museum was the inspiration of the 1st Viscount Harcourt and the 2nd Viscount Esher. It was to be for London what the Carnavalet Museum was for Paris, a museum to show the rich cultural history of London in its widest sense. Everything was to be there: antiquities, paintings and works of art to illustrate the whole metropolis within twenty miles of Charing Cross. It was given what was for a museum unprecedented publicity in advance of its opening at Kensington Palace on 8 April 1912. Admission of the public was delayed by the threat of violence from the Suffragettes – who are well represented by material in the present museum collections. Guy Laking, the first Keeper of the London Museum, had a considerable flair for showmanship and the new Museum reacted against the approach of traditional museums. Accordingly, the London Museum included some spectacular models, acquired from the Franco-British exhibition at White City in 1908 and 1909. The illuminated tableau of the Great Fire of 1666 may well have been one of them, and is still on show today.

The new London Museum forgot the existence of the Guildhall Museum. It also had a buccaneering attitude to collecting. By means of financial inducements, it succeeded in persuading George Lawrence, who had previously collected objects from building sites for the Guildhall, to acquire Roman and other objects for the London Museum. Such poaching made a clash between the two Museums almost inevitable, and it came in 1912 over the Cheapside Hoard.

In 1912, workmen demolishing an old shop in Cheapside, opposite the church of St Mary-le-Bow, discovered the remains of a wooden box, filled with jewellery dating from about the end of the sixteenth century. George Lawrence acted quickly. By going round the public houses frequented by these workmen, he managed to buy from them, at a modest price, the whole collection. It was then purchased by the London Museum and put on exhibition. When the news reached the ears of the Guildhall Museum authorities, action was taken on the grounds that this jewellery, which included some gold and silver, was Treasure Trove. Treasure Trove is 'Gold or Silver, hidden in the earth with a view to recovery, of which the present owner is unknown.' Normally such treasure belongs to the Crown, but the City of London is among a small number of bodies to which a franchise has been granted. Thus Treasure Trove found within the City or its liberties passes to 'the Mayor and Commonalty and citizens and their successors.' A somewhat acrimonious correspondence followed between the London Museum and the Corporation of London, but finally a compromise was reached, by which the London Museum presented the Guildhall Museum with about a third of the collection, free of charge. One third also went to the Victoria and Albert Museum. With the amalgamation of the London and Guildhall Museums, two-thirds of the hoard are now re-united and on display.

In 1914, the London Museum moved to Lancaster House and a proper home. Lord Leverhulme gave the unexpired portion of the lease of the house for the purposes of the Museum. Here, the London Museum developed its principles, which still continues, of collecting all relevant classes of material, from every period.

Model of the Great Fire of 1666
Probably made by Thorp of London, c. 1908, and refurbished by them in 1975
'Guy Laking's new Museum', wrote Sir Mortimer Wheeler in 1937, 'was an implicit reaction to the formal, static collections of the traditional sort. Thus, the Great Fire of London was represented, not merely by charred fragments in a glass case, but by a working model in which, by ingenious electrical contrivances, flames leapt about the Old St Paul's amidst rolling clouds of smoke.'
(Twenty-five Years of the London Museum.)

Walter H. Lambert (1870–1950)
Popularity: The Stars of the Edwardian Music Hall
1901-03; oil on canvas; 1600 × 3769mm
A group portrait of the principal music-hall artists at the turn of the century. It shows 231 performers, including Harry Lauder, Dan Leno, Marie Lloyd, Little Tich – and the artist himself in his professional role as the female impersonator Lydia Dreams (foreground left, above the sandwich-board man.). The setting is outside the Old Vic in Waterloo Road, looking north towards Waterloo Station.

(Left) **Head of the god Mithras**
Late 2nd – 3rd century; from the Temple of Mithras in Walbrook; imported marble; height 350mm
The Temple of Mithras was discovered in 1954 during the building of Bucklersbury House, between Bank and Cannon Street. The head had been deliberately buried in the 4th century, perhaps to escape discovery after the adoption of Christianity as the official religion. A campaign to preserve the remains of the temple caused a considerable furore, highlighting the threat to archaeology by redevelopment in the City. The temple was eventually moved further west, to the forecourt of Temple Court.

(Opposite) **The industry and commerce collection**
Situated in the London Docklands is the Museum's store of material bearing on all aspects of the port, trade and industry of London. The position of London at the centre of the Empire made it at once the warehouse and workshop of the world. Here are the means of handling imports – bales, barrels, scales and cranes – all awaiting display in the new Museum of London in Docklands planned to open in 1988.

Two Directors: Mr Tom Hume and Sir Mortimer Wheeler at the laying of the foundation stone of the new Museum of London by Her Majesty Queen Elizabeth The Queen Mother on 29 March 1973
R.E.M. Wheeler, as he then was, was Keeper of the London Museum from 1926 to 1944. Tom Hume, who became Director of the Museum of London in 1972, saw the new Museum through to completion and opening before he retired in 1977.

The acquisition of contemporary material such as a hansom cab, while there were still a few such vehicles in the streets, was regarded as novel. It was not to be an art museum. It pioneered new areas, such as costume and dress, not for the sake of collecting, but because such objects reflected, in the words of the archaeologist Sir Mortimer Wheeler (who became Keeper in 1926), a 'response to the environment or to the ordinary evolutionary processes of the mind.' As well as showing a rather unexpected interest in costume, Wheeler was instrumental in putting the study of the archaeology of London onto a much sounder base, drawing on the collections of both the Guildhall and London Museums for this purpose.

It was under Wheeler in 1927 that the first suggestion was put forward that the two Museums should be amalgamated. But the idea was not to be pursued until after the Second World War. This left both the Guildhall and London Museums without their homes, not because of bomb damage but because the Corporation and Government each decided to use the premises of their Museums for other purposes. Eventually, temporary premises were found for both: the London Museum reopened once more in Kensington Palace in 1951 and the Guildhall Museum opened in the Royal Exchange in the City in 1955. These arrangements were not satisfactory, and in 1959 the Government explored the suggestion that the two Museums be amalgamated in a new building on a site to be made available by the Corporation. Although the necessary legislation was passed in 1965, problems of finance delayed the start of the new building until 1971. The new Museum, known as the Museum of London, is now jointly funded by national and local government and administered by a Board of Governors appointed by both sides.

The Museum of London is very much greater than the two original Museums. It has bigger collections (enormous amounts of material have been added since 1976), a bigger building, a bigger staff and, above all, a bigger audience. But visitors see only a small proportion of the activity of the Museum as they walk round the galleries, attend a lecture or workshop given by a specialist, or enjoy a film. Most of the effort of the staff (there are over 200) is geared to ensuring that those who come receive the best possible experience from their visit. To do this, the Museum must create the right collections, carry out research upon them and provide an agreeable environment.

A great many of the new items acquired by the Museum are derived from fieldwork. There is a very large programme of excavation throughout Greater London undertaken by or co-ordinated from the Museum. Over seventy people are employed, examining all redevelopment sites in London where important prehistoric, Roman, or medieval remains might be expected. There is also an extensive programme to record industry and other aspects of life in London since the sixteenth century. The results of these activities (objects, field notes, photographs, plans, tape-recordings) are incorporated in the collections where they can be used by the Museum's own staff for publications,

exhibitions and educational programmes and by anyone else who needs them. The Museum also buys objects from time to time and receives many gifts from individuals and companies. However, before you offer us yet another vacuum cleaner, it is worth stating why we do not accept every potential donation.

The vastness of London has already been mentioned; the Museum could easily accept almost any object on the grounds that it has a London connection, or perhaps represents some stage in the technical evolution of an object made in London. The Museum, therefore, must discriminate most carefully if it is not to be overwhelmed. In making a decision about whether to accept an object, great emphasis is placed on the context from which it comes, or, if that is not specially significant, the context in the Museum into which it will fit. For instance, it is unlikely that a piece of broken pottery will be of use to the archaeological collections unless the precise deposit from which it comes is known. On the other hand, a medieval pilgrim badge found on the foreshore of the Thames without a clear archaeological association might well be significant when fitted into the context of a range of materials already in the Museum, illustrating London craftsmanship of the period. Similarly, in the twentieth century, selective additions of costume may enhance the Museum's ability to show the range of products of the dressmaker. The opportunity to acquire a whole workshop, however, together with film and sound records of how it was used, can provide a complete insight into working life – one that is unobtainable for earlier centuries.

The Museum of London is a dynamic institution still expanding and developing its role. Immense new opportunities to improve its services now present themselves, as film, sound and video records of London are obtained and laid down, like wine, for future use. A museum in the Isle of Dogs, a gallery for paintings, prints and drawings, and another for dress are planned for the future. But the central core of our activity is at London Wall. In the pages which follow you can see some of the highlights from the story of London – perhaps the greatest city in the world.

MAX HEBDITCH
Director

Bringing history alive

(Above) *Two members of an historical dance group, dressed in period costume, perform a sequence of late-17th-century dances in the Museum galleries. (Above right) A group of schoolchildren attend a lecture at the Museum, whose Education Department receives over 2,000 school groups each year. (Right) Part of the vast store of costumes and textiles, one of the largest specialist areas of the Museum. Items are drawn from here to maintain the permanent exhibitions and provide special shows, as well as being a rich source for research.*

Prehistoric and Roman London

The amalgamation of the London and Guildhall Museums provided this department with a comprehensive and wide-ranging collection. While the strength of the London Museum lay in its prehistoric material, particularly in the bronze age metalwork from the River Thames, the Guildhall Museum's Roman antiquities, resulting from continued acquisitions from sites in the City of London since the mid nineteenth century, had long been regarded as one of the most important collections in Britain.

In the galleries, these collections are used to recount the London story from the arrival of palaeolithic hunter-gatherers over 250,000 years ago, finishing with the collapse of Roman authority in the early fifth century AD. The natural background – the geology and pre-agricultural vegetation of the Thames valley – is indicated. The prehistoric display shows how the valley of the Lower Thames provided a homeland successively for palaeolithic, mesolithic, neolithic, bronze and iron age peoples, and illustrates the roles the Thames played as a highway, a tribal boundary and, probably, a sacred river. An array of bronze weapons and tools is evidence of large-scale bronze working in Greater London.

The Roman gallery sketches the history of *Londinium* from its birth after the Roman invasion of AD 43, through its development into a flourishing commercial and administrative capital, to the final withdrawal of central authority in AD 410. Within this framework social and economic themes and aspects of daily life are fully explored and illustrated. To achieve this comprehensive picture of life through four centuries a variety of display techniques are used, ranging from traditional case layouts to reconstructions of portions of three Roman rooms which, together with the substantial mosaic pavement found in Bucklersbury in 1869, now relaid and restored, form the gallery's central feature.

Disruption of the historic landscape, whether by gravel quarrying, river dredging, road building or property development, has in the past, and increasingly today, led to the discovery of prehistoric and Roman artefacts in the London area. In the second half of the nineteenth century and the first half of the twentieth, random collection by interested individual antiquaries was the most common source of finds. Thus the department holds a major collection of 2,700 palaeolithic flint implements ranging in date from 300,000 to 70,000 years old, found by Robert Garraway Rice between 1905 and 1929 in gravel pits at Yiewsley, West London.

Since the Thames was the main highway into Britain for prehistoric settlers and traders, linking it with central Europe via the Rhine, it provided a route for introducing technical innovations into Britain. The bronze swords in the collection, recovered from the Thames, are examples of a unique series of imported implements and of the close copies made in the London area.

Roman dining-room
c. 100 AD (reconstruction); metal, ceramic and glass items found on various sites in the City; furniture reconstructed on the basis of evidence from London and elsewhere
This dining-room indicates the reliance on trade from other parts of the Empire during the early years of Roman occupation. London was a cosmopolitan city, and those immigrants settling in London demanded the luxuries to which they were accustomed. The red gloss tableware (samian ware) was an early example of mass production. Made in France, it was exported all over the Empire. By the 2nd century AD, however, centres of local production had grown up, making the province more self reliant.

The dramatic growth of organized field archaeology over the last forty years, not least within the area of the walled city of Roman London, has not only increased the manifold riches of the collection, but has also ensured by stratigraphical study that the date and nature of the deposit surrounding the object is known and recorded. In terms of Roman material, the excavations of bomb-sites in the City after the Second World War produced the department's most prized objects: the cache of marble sculptures and the ornate silver ritual casket from the Temple of Mithras. Three additional sculptured pieces, found in the same area in 1889 and displayed in the London Museum, were re-united with the new finds to form a unique collection of Roman religious statuary.

From the small River Walbrook adjacent to the Temple site came a mass of everyday domestic objects; craft tools made of iron and bronze, objects of tin, wood, leather and organic materials, all perfectly preserved in the riverine deposits. These and other personal objects recovered either in the last hundred years or now by systematic excavation from similar well-preserved deposits, characterize the quality of the collection and the unrivalled range of material with which to illustrate the life of the busy cosmopolitan trading emporium that was Roman London.

Jadeite axehead
Neolithic (c. 3000 BC); 163 × 71 mm; from the Thames at Mortlake
Polishing flint and stone axeheads to improve their cutting properties was one of the technological advances adopted in Britain when farming was introduced, in about 4000 BC. Jadeite is not found in the British Isles, but was frequently imported from the Alps or Northern Italy. The axehead is thus probably one of the earliest known foreign imports into the London area. It may have been a ritual object.

Mesolithic hunter's shelter
c. 8000 – 4000 BC (reconstruction); implements from localities in Greater London
A late summer scene in the shelter of a family of hunters and food gatherers near a tributary of the Thames in the London area, some time between the end of the last ice age and the introduction of farming. The equipment includes chipped flint axes for woodworking, small flint tools, flint waste from tool making, barbed antler spearheads for hunting or fishing and a weighted stick for digging up edible plants.

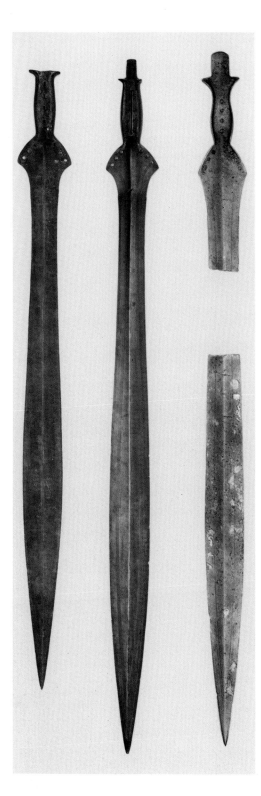

Iron dagger and sheath

Iron age (*c.* 550 BC); sheath of bronze strips wrapped around wooden lining; 358 × 100mm; probably from the Thames at Mortlake (Layton Collection)

One of the earliest known iron artefacts from Britain, this is a luxury weapon for a tribal chief. It is one of a series of similar weapons from the Thames in West London. The dagger could be an import from the Continent, but the construction details of the elaborate sheath show this to be British, and illustrate the continuity with local bronze age methods of manufacture.

The Brentford Tankard

Iron age (1st century BC – 1st century AD); oak staves encased in three bronze bands, with small bronze handle; height 146mm, diameter of rim 165mm, capacity *c.* 2.3 litres; probably from the Thames at Brentford or Kew (Layton Collection)

The Celtic-speaking tribes who dominated southeastern Britain at the end of the iron age evidently delighted in feasting and drinking, and this tankard may have held the native drink, beer. To drink from it, one probably grasped it with both hands, slipping one or two fingers of the right hand under the handle or 'holdfast'.

(Left) Bronze swords

Bronze age (*c.* 1000 BC); lengths (left to right) 745, 801 and 716mm; from the Thames at Battersea, Millwall and Wandsworth

By about 1200 BC a vigorous bronze-working industry had evidently grown up in the Thames valley, and these swords are among hundreds of fine bronze implements recovered from the river. The one on the left was a revolutionary new type of weapon introduced from the Continent, and the others are local adaptations.

Pointed handaxe

Lower Palaeolithic (c. 250,000 BC); chipped from a flint nodule;
200 × 100mm; found in 1913 with nine other handaxes on the site
of the Regent Palace Hotel near Piccadilly Circus
*Handaxes were probably used for butchering animal carcasses and for
other cutting, smashing and piercing jobs. They seem usually to have been
held in the hand, by the wide end. Thousands of handaxes have been
found in the Thames valley, made by bands of hunters and food gatherers
living there during a temperate period between two ice ages.*

Roman Mithraic relief

3rd century AD; Italian marble found in Walbrook in 1889,
probably part of the Mithraic temple excavated in 1954 (see p. 8)
*Mithras is seen here stabbing the bull from whose blood springs all earthly
life. He is accompanied by the torch bearers Cautes and Cautopates.
Signs of the zodiac and gods frame the relief. This work, erected in
fulfilment of a vow, would have been viewed only by initiates of Mithras.
The cults of Mithras and Isis were brought to London by the Romans and
gained great popularity, offering greater emotional satisfaction through
their belief in the after-life than the traditional Graeco-Roman religions.*

Necklaces of amber and emerald beads

1st – 2nd century AD; amber threaded on flax, 439mm, from Old Jewry; emerald on fine gold wire, 110mm, from Cannon Street

Amber was transported by the Romans over land from the east coast of the Baltic to North Italy (Aquileia) for manufacture into jewellery, which was re-exported to other parts of the Empire. The emerald beads, straight sided and hexagonal in section, also illustrate London's long-distance trade connections, for their likely source is Egypt.

Model of the port of Roman London

c. 100 AD (reconstruction); scale 1:72; 1400 × 1100mm

This model is based on evidence from excavations in 1981, which uncovered a timber bridge pier, a massive timber-faced quay and warehouses. The choice of this site for London, on a navigable river linked to the North Sea and Europe, ensured that only fifty years after its foundation in 50 AD it had become the busiest trading emporium in the province of Britain.

Romano-British pottery

1st – 2nd century AD; from numerous sites

Local kilns provided both utilitarian and fine-ware vessels for Roman London. At Highgate Woods, three miles north-west of the city, potteries produced grey-ware 'poppy-head' beakers (back row, left). The mortarium (below left), with a gritted surface for grinding, was made at Brockley Hill, twelve miles from London, while kilns in Kent fired the roughly made cooking pot in clay with a high shell content (centre).

Cutler's stall

c. 100 AD (reconstruction)

Based on a contemporary sculptured relief from Ostia, Italy, this display represents the upper part of a portable stall used by a street trader of knives and other edged tools. With the exception of the replica bundles in the centre, the knives, shears, pruning hooks and specialist curriers' blades are finds from the Roman city. Most are of iron with bronze or bone handles.

(Left) Carpenter's bench

50 – 100 AD (reconstruction); tools mostly found in the Roman levels of the River Walbrook

The waterlogged deposits of the Walbrook valley, in the central area of the City, have yielded many Roman metal tools, preserved in perfect condition. Their original disposition may have been through casual loss or religious offering. Here, carpenter's tools, very similar to their modern counterparts, have been assembled: chisels, awls, drill bits, an axe, draw-knives and hand-saws. They have been fitted with modern handles, and are all of iron, except the folding rule which is of bronze and measures 1 Roman foot.

Legionary soldier
Late 1st – early 2nd century AD; stone;
height 1320mm; originally from a tomb,
but found built into a bastion of the city
wall in Camomile Street, just east of
London Wall

*The figure is wearing a tunic and cloak, with a short
sword and studded strap hanging from his belt. His
left hand holds a case of wooden writing tablets,
suggesting that his duties were partly clerical. The
Roman army in London probably performed an
administrative rather than a military role, and this
soldier could well have been a non-commissioned
officer, seconded from his legion to serve the
headquarters staff of the Governor.*

Inscribed altar
Mid 3rd century AD; Barnack stone
(limestone); height 1220mm; found re-used in
a late Roman riverside defensive wall at
Blackfriars
*The inscription records the rebuilding, after decay
or collapse, of a temple to the Egyptian goddess Isis.
Oriental and Egyptian divinities had become
increasingly popular throughout the Roman Empire
by the 3rd century AD. The site of the temple is not
known, but it probably formed part of a complex of
secular and religious public buildings in the south-
west corner of the Roman city. The altar was
dedicated by Marcus Martiannius Pulcher,
Governor of the province of Upper Britain from
251 to 259 AD.*

Medieval London

The department spans a thousand years, from the obscurity and silence of 'dark age' London in the fifth century AD, to the colour and clamour of the fifteenth-century capital, a city full of life, not yet scattered to distant suburbs, and a community proudly regarding itself as 'a mirror to all England' and 'watch-tower of the realm'. The galleries dealing with this long period illustrate London's chequered rise to pre-eminence not only as the seat of the nation's Government but as the magnet of society and fashion and as the primary centre of industry and international trade. By the time of Geoffrey Chaucer (1340-1400), best known of all medieval Londoners, the city had enough importance and appeal to draw together all those elements of English society described in the Prologue to his *Canterbury Tales*.

The remarkable diversity of objects that have survived in London's soil from this period, particularly from the thirteenth century onwards, helps to evoke most aspects of life in the medieval city, including its sharp contrasts; pollution and violence, for example, alongside secular and ecclesiastical wealth.

Here, as throughout the Museum's displays, only a small part of the collection can remain permanently on show, the reserve being regularly drawn upon for temporary exhibitions, book illustrations and the like, and kept accessible for research of all kinds. Thus the collection of medieval pottery, probably the largest in Europe, is not only a repository of information widely consulted by archaeologists and social historians, but a source of inspiration to potters of today.

The establishment of the Museum of London united two roughly equal, complementary medieval collections. That both the Guildhall Museum and the London Museum had managed to build up such worthwhile endowments may be surprising, given that it is only during the last two or three decades that medieval archaeology has become generally accepted as a subject of serious study and that medieval artefacts have begun to excite the same level of interest as relics of the Roman period. It was perhaps inevitable that in the nineteenth century a few important collections of medieval material from London should go by default to the British Museum and various provincial museums. Nevertheless the Guildhall Museum, long before the publication of its catalogue in 1903, had quietly accumulated a fine stock of medieval antiquities, representing a fair proportion of those objects rescued during building work on city sites. These ranged from the decorated thirteenth-century stone coffin of Godfrey the Trumpeter to a hoard of silver coins of Edward the Confessor and William the Conqueror, or the bone skates, leather shoes and metalwork from the medieval marsh around Moorfields and London Wall. The early panache and persistence of the London Museum, on the other hand, were to attract to it many groups of chance finds still remaining in private hands. These provided an impressive base for its medieval displays and eventually for the invaluable catalogues of the Saxon, Viking and medieval material published between 1927 and 1940.

Panel from a chest
c. 1400; elm; 5250 × 1030mm
Though incomplete, the carving shows part of the story – a sermon on the consequences of greed – told by the Pardoner in Chaucer's Canterbury Tales. In a time of plague, three men-about-town swear to find Death and destroy him. Instead they discover a heap of gold, which two guard while the third goes to find food and drink. Planning to kill his companions for their share of the gold, he buys poison from an apothecary (left) and mixes it with wine. On his return his friends, similarly minded, set upon him and kill him (centre). They decide to celebrate, unwittingly drink the poisoned wine and perish also.

A large percentage of the collections was recovered from the Thames. Quantities of Anglo-Saxon weapons, for instance, were dredged from the river in the western parts of modern London. In the City, on the other hand, the rebuilding of wharves in Victorian times yielded rich concentrations of later medieval material, and the major development of this same area in the 1970s and 1980s provided the opportunity for a series of excavations and observations by the Museum's archaeological staff. This recent work, while making significant additions to the stock of medieval antiquities, has contributed most by establishing scientific dating evidence and consequently a more objective and more accurate framework for the collections as a whole. Even so, chance still continues to play its part, for modern exponents of the time-honoured tradition of 'mudlarking' for antiquities on the Thames foreshore have been responsible for discovering some of the most outstanding recent acquisitions.

Silver penny and halfpenny
c. 886 (penny) and c. 959-73 (halfpenny); diameters 18mm and 15mm
These two coins were both minted in London, and on their reverses have monograms made from the name '*LONDINIA*'. *The penny (left) may have been struck to celebrate Alfred's reoccupation of London during his war with the Danes, who controlled most of eastern England. King Edgar's halfpenny, a recent find, is extremely rare.*

Group of weapons from London Bridge
Early 11th century (modern handles); width of largest axehead 200mm
These iron spear-heads and elegant battle-axes are of the type used by the Danish invaders during the wars which culminated in the accession of the Danish King Cnut (Canute) to the throne of England. London, and in particular its bridge which barred the Thames to Danish fleets, was the centre of much of the warfare.

(Opposite) **Decorated stone slab**
c. 1030; limestone; 470 × 540mm
Decorated in the 'Ringerike' style developed in late Anglo-Saxon England under Scandinavian influence, the stone shows a stylized lion fighting a serpent, with traces of painted colour still visible on the surface. An inscription on one end, in Old Norse runes, records that it was set up by 'Ginna' and 'Toki'. Found in St Paul's Church Yard, it probably formed part of a tomb, perhaps of one of the Scandinavian nobles at the court of King Cnut.

Pottery

Late 13th – early 14th century; made in London, Kingston (Surrey), Mill Green (Essex) and the Saintonge region of south-west France (polychrome jug); all found in London

The medieval potter's art was at its height during the late 13th and 14th centuries, when medieval London itself was probably at its most populous and prosperous. This selection includes jugs for serving wine or water, anthropomorphic vessels used perhaps for convivial drinking, and a double-sectioned condiment dish for presenting food at table.

Medieval kitchen

This room setting includes cooking vessels, jugs made of bronze (which in the later Middle Ages was becoming more common and replacing pottery) and a pewter plate on the shelf at the back, which represents the sort of fine metalware increasingly to be found on tables alongside the more common turned wooden bowls. On the right-hand side of the middle shelf is a quern or handmill used for grinding flour for bread or malt to make ale.

Anglo-Saxon brooch

6th century; silver-gilt; length 100mm

This heavy brooch, cast in silver with an intricate interlace design, and gilded over most of its front surface, was found with a burial in an Anglo-Saxon cemetery at Mitcham in Surrey. It is the finest piece of early Anglo-Saxon jewellery to have been found in the London area, which at that date was not densely settled.

Bell
c. 1340; copper alloy; inscribed 'PETRVS DE
VESTON ME FECIT' ('Peter de Weston made
me'); height 438mm
*Peter de Weston worked near Aldgate, the
centre of medieval London's 'heavy' industry.
In his time he was one of the city's chief bell-
founders, handling commissions from all over
south-east England. He also catered for the
growing demand for bronze cooking-pots and
table vessels, and may have had a hand in
casting some of the earliest cannon, used at the
siege of Calais in 1346.*

(Opposite) **Hanging lamp**
12th century; bronze; height 310mm
*Recovered from the site of St Martin's le Grand, a
collegiate church and sanctuary which stood within
the city walls near Aldersgate, this lamp was
designed to take six oil-burning wicks and may have
hung above the high altar.*

Pilgrim badges

Late 14th century; pewter; height of ship 75mm

These are souvenirs brought back by pilgrims who, in the time of Chaucer, had visited Canterbury Cathedral, the scene of the martyrdom of Archbishop Thomas Becket in 1170. The ship badge commemorates Becket's return from exile a month before his murder. The badge of the murder weapon represents one of the stations in the pilgrim's tour of Canterbury Cathedral. Becket was himself a Londoner and, after his martyrdom, was regarded as the city's special protector.

Document bags

14th century; cordwain (tawed hide); width of larger bag 640mm

The smaller bag was made in 1348 to hold the accounts submitted to the Royal Exchequer at Westminster that year by William Shrewsbury, treasurer of the English garrison at Calais. In the other bag were filed the accounts of King Richard II's officials in the county palatine of Chester and the county of Flint in 1394. The demand for products of leather and skin, from shoes to parchment, gave rise to many specialized crafts in London's important leather industry.

Straight trumpet
14th century; copper alloy

This trumpet, found at Billingsgate in 1984, is an extremely rare example of a high-quality medieval wind instrument. Almost as tall as the man who once blew it, the trumpet is remarkably light in weight and can be instantly dismantled into four convenient sections. Made from twenty pieces of sheet metal by a highly specialized craftsman, the trumpet is one of the most complex medieval objects yet found in London. Aside from music-making, it may have been used for sounding commands and signals, on board ship, for example.

Enamelled glass beaker
13th – early 14th century; possibly Venetian; height 95mm

Part of a beaker of fine clear glass, decorated in coloured enamels with heraldic lions and shields, and one of a group of at least six similar glasses found in 1982 during excavations in Foster Lane, just south of the Museum. Glasses like this were obviously very valuable, and were commissioned from specialist craftsmen, possibly in Venice. Only a few other fragments are known from elsewhere in the British Isles; the Foster Lane discovery represents the largest group yet found anywhere in Europe.

(Opposite) Cradle
Late 15th century; oak; 1800 × 860 × 710mm (including stand)

A rare survival, this would have been the night cradle of a high-born infant. It has slots near the top to take swaddling bands over the baby's coverlets, and hangs by iron hooks and rings from chamfered posts.

Seal matrices and impressions

(*Left*) The seal of Thomas Barry, Bishop of Ossory (Kilkenny, Ireland); *c.* 1427; copper alloy; length 72mm; from the Thames at Vintners' Hall. (*Right*) The seal of the Brewers' Company of London; mid 15th century; silver; diameter 63mm

Seal dies and impressions are almost all that survive of the loosely organized craft of seal engraving, which like many other specialities was overlooked when the Brewers' clerk listed 111 crafts in London in 1422. Thomas Barry's seal depicts the enthroned figure of the 7th-century Irish St Canice beneath the Trinity and between the arms of Ormonde and Barry. The Brewers' company seal shows the Assumption of the Virgin, in a rayed aureole, with God the Father above.

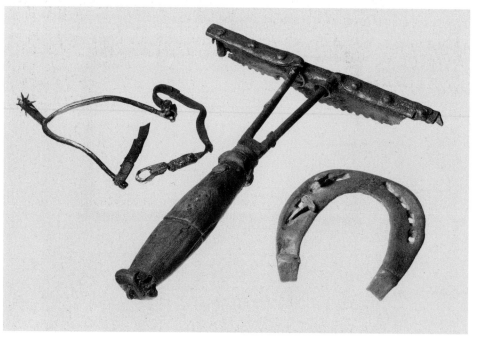

Spur, curry comb and horseshoe

Late 13th century; wood, iron and leather; length of horseshoe 120mm

The curry comb (centre), with its alder handle, would have been used in the grooming of horses. The spur illustrates technological change: the introduction of the rowel in place of a fixed spike. The spur's tinned surfaces and fittings, on the other hand, demonstrate the strength of craft traditions, for London spurriers flashed their iron wares with tin from Saxon times onwards.

SS collar

c. 1440–50; silver; length c. 210mm
*Recovered from the Thames, this is perhaps the
only surviving medieval example of the livery
introduced by the royal House of Lancaster and
bestowed by Henry IV, Henry V and Henry VI on
those they wished to honour, and which is
represented by the letters SS. These are thought to
stand for souveigne vous de moi, 'forget me not',
or sovereyne, 'sovereign lady', probably the Virgin
Mary. From its fluted ring would have hung a royal
or family badge. The effigy of John Gower, the
court poet, in Southwark Cathedral, wears an SS
collar with the swan badge used by Henry IV.*

Infant's footwear and toy

14th century; leather and pewter; length of
shoe 125mm; height of toy 28mm
*This well-worn little half-boot, from the late-14th-
century backfill of Baynard's Castle Dock (near
the Mermaid Theatre) is typical of most medieval
footwear: lightweight, flexible and short-lived, with
a thin, shapely sole and no raised heel. The toy
song-bird is one of many sophisticated playthings
recently recovered from the soil of medieval
London.*

Tudor and Stuart London

Between 1500 and 1600, life in London changed dramatically. The population grew from about 50,000 to 200,000 and the city became desperately overcrowded. During his reign (1509-47) Henry VIII encouraged immigration from Europe, established new industries and dissolved the religious houses. Under Queen Elizabeth (1558-1603), London became a major European market and port, trading with America, Africa and the Far East.

From 1600 to 1660 London's population increased from some 200,000 to 400,000. Inigo Jones changed the Gothic appearance of the city with his Italianate buildings of brick and stone at Covent Garden (London's first square), the Banqueting House, Whitehall, and the refacing of St Paul's Cathedral. Citizens now had piped water in their homes and permanent theatres to attend on Bankside, Southwark. The Civil War made London the setting for two great political events, the trial and beheading of the King. Fire and disease remained the greatest hazards: the plague of 1665 killed one in three Londoners, and in the Great Fire of 1666 four-fifths of the city was destroyed.

Although new houses had to conform to building regulations, the opportunity to create a new city was lost, and London's medieval layout was preserved. The City, no longer the main residential area, developed as a commercial and financial centre. The Bank of England was established in 1694, and new industries such as silk weaving in nearby Spitalfields reflected the improving quality of life. Trade with the Far East introduced tea and coffee, and the establishment of coffee houses provided convivial meeting places for the exchange of social, political and business news.

Regular coach and postal services, on improved turnpike (toll) roads, disseminated news and ideas from London. By 1700 the population was about 680,000.

The collections maintained by the Tudor and Stuart department reflect the life led by Londoners of the period, with respect both to its increased variety and many hardships. Amalgamation of the London and Guildhall museums brought together two of the best collections of early modern English ceramics; over 3,000 pieces of earthenware, stoneware, slipware and tin-glaze. To the department's metalwork collection, with its numerous items of domestic pewter, weapons, cutlery and personal accessories, have been added several outstanding pieces from the Thames foreshore, found by 'mudlarks'. The W.G. Bell and Sir Richard Tangye collections of contemporary books and manuscripts acquired by the London Museum in 1942 and 1946 record the Great Fire and Plague of London, and the Cromwellian interregnum. The Fire is also represented by a model, which shows the vast area affected.

In the Tudor gallery, particular attention is paid to products that had formerly been imported from abroad but were now imitated by London makers. These include delftware, a type of tin-glaze originating from the Netherlands, now imitated at Aldgate, and clear crystal glass, formerly only made in Venice, but now produced at Crutched Friars near the Tower. Clocks and watches were made by the Dutch communities in Austin Friars, near Broad Street in the City, and St Martin-in-the-Fields and Greenwich, established by Henry VIII, using German and Italian craftsmen.

The Cheapside Hoard
c. 1580–1620; from a Jacobean goldsmith's stock-in-trade, found in 1912 under a cellar floor in Cheapside
The collection is typical of Elizabethan jewellery, with many bright stones in simple enamelled settings, toadstones (fossil fish teeth) which were believed to have medicinal properties, and partially cut gemstones and cameos. The crystal tankard and salt-cellar were almost certainly pawns or pledges, while the large Colombian emerald has been hollowed out to take a watch movement.

The indigenous craft of fine goldsmithing is represented by the Cheapside Hoard, the country's largest hoard of jewellery, and the silver-gilt mounts of the courtly Parr Pot. Developments in international trade encouraged the foundation of the Royal Exchange in 1570, by Sir Thomas Gresham, economic adviser to the Crown, whose steelyard was probably made for the new institution.

New material from excavation plays a vital role in the growth of our knowledge of sixteenth- and seventeenth-century London life. Apart from many random finds, several important groups from building sites were recovered by the London and Guildhall museums, notably the rarely surviving clothes worn by ordinary people and found in marshy deposits in Moorfields (flat, knitted caps, hose and leather shoes). Several important groups of glass, both indigenous and imported, from Gracechurch Street and other sites, provide valuable comparative material.

Finds from the royal palace sites – Whitehall, Nonsuch (in Surrey) and the Tower – form a major part of the department's reserve collections. The material from these sites is mainly well-dated ceramic groups, and architectural fragments – in the case of Nonsuch, 6,000 pieces of carved plaster.

A large variety of domestic articles – ceramics, pewter, plate and small metalwork – illustrates the development of fashionable London in the seventeenth century, alongside built-in architectural exhibits such as the Wandsworth and Poyle Park period rooms. The collections boast many fine London watches and scientific instruments (examples of two important new local industries), while trumpets by Augustine Dudley (1651 and 1666) and William Bull (late seventeenth century) are amongst the earliest known English examples. The recent acquisition of four splendid marble ships from the Trinity Hospital, Mile End Road, serve as a reminder of the prominence of the navy and the importance of ship-building in Stuart times. The Hounslow sword factory of the late 1630s and early 1640s is represented by an important collection of swords.

Of the 437 pieces comprising the Garton Glass Collection, presented to the London Museum in 1943, the most important are the mid-seventeenth-century Scudamore Flute, two giant late-seventeenth-century ceremonial goblets, à la façon de Venise, and examples by George Ravenscroft, showing the new improved lead glass technology of the late seventeenth century.

An advance in ceramics technology is also demonstrated by the Fulham Pottery excavation material donated in 1982, which includes examples of John Dwight's stoneware bellarmine production, his experimental porcelain, and the earliest known English red stoneware teapot, c. 1675. Of the material relating to late-seventeenth-century overseas trade, pride of place must be given to the South Sea Company silver-gilt cup and salver of 1715, purchased in 1983.

Finally, to remedy the lack of physical evidence of London's early modern industrial activities, a clay pipe kiln, c. 1680, excavated in Southwark by the Southwark and Lambeth Archaeological Unit, was moved to the Museum under the supervision of the Museum's Conservation Department, and is now on display in the Stuart galleries.

Steelyard (weigh-beam)
Dated 1572 on shield; weight above hook inscribed 'THOMAS GRESHAM LONDON'; length 980mm

This steelyard may well have been one of the fittings provided for the merchants using Gresham's Royal Exchange. The first national standards for weighing and measuring were established by Henry VII, who distributed uniform metal weights and measures to every borough. The two armed figures, possibly representing Gog and Magog, and the dragon and boy, are 17th-century additions.

Carved plaster
1538–45; height 190mm; from Nonsuch Palace, Surrey (now demolished)
Italian and French plasterers trained by Primaticcio at Fontainebleau were employed for the decoration of Nonsuch Palace. Classical elements in carving such as this were most unusual in England before the early 17th century.

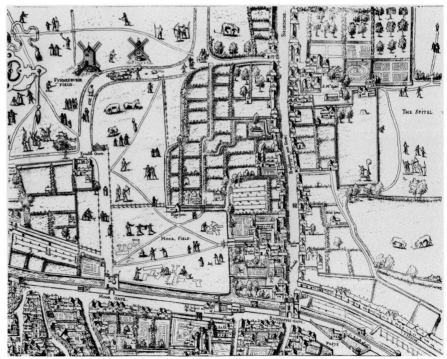

Engraved copper plate of a map of the Moorfields area, *c.* 1558, with a modern print from it

370 × 502mm

One of perhaps twenty copper sheets which made up the earliest map of London, of which no original copies survive. On the reverse of the plate is an oil painting of the Tower of Babel by Martin van Valckenborgh, c. 1595. One other plate is known, showing the City, also with an oil on the reverse. The worn plates were presumably exported to the Low Countries, where artists preferred to paint on copper.

Tin-glazed plate
1602; inscription in praise of Elizabeth I; diameter 260mm
This plate, probably made by a Flemish potter at Aldgate, is the earliest known dated piece of English delft (tin-glazed earthenware). The brilliant colours of tin-glaze, a technique new to England, imitated those of oriental porcelain and contrasted with the soft browns and greens of traditional English lead-glazed earthenware.

The Parr Pot
Hallmarked 1546/47; white-striped (latticino) glass with English silver-gilt mounts, enamelled with the arms of William Parr, uncle and chamberlain to Queen Katherine; height 150mm
In the 16th century the technique of making latticino glass was known only to Italian glass-makers, and there was great competition among European monarchs to attract them to their courts. In the 1540s six Venetians were working in London, and Henry VIII had about nineteen drinking glasses, some mounted in silver-gilt.

The Great Plague, 1665
Bubonic plague afflicted the city particularly severely in 1665, killing almost one in three Londoners. Apothecary jars and phials contained antidotes such as London 'treacle', a compound of oil, gunpowder and sack (sherry). The plague bell was rung to announce the corpse collector. Weekly Bills of Mortality were compiled by the Parish clerk: this special edition lists all recorded deaths in 1665.

Late Stuart interior

Pinewood panelling from Poyle Park, Tongham, Surrey (now demolished), mid 17th century; painted ceiling showing Summer personified, oil on plaster, c. 1676-77, from 15 Buckingham Street, off the Strand; virginals, signed 'Jacobus White fecit', dated 1656, made in Old Jewry; black lacquer screen; stained wood cabinet, veneered in tortoiseshell, Flemish, c. 1680

The panelling was probably commissioned by the grandson of Sir Nicholas Woodroffe, a distinguished London merchant who bought Poyle Park in 1582. The furniture represents the taste of a prosperous Stuart merchant and includes a lacquer screen, with Chinese motifs showing the influence on London furnishings of the East India Company's trade.

Samuel Pepys's chess board

c. 1680; board inlaid with various woods and ivory; pieces in ivory; 550 × 625mm

Originally given to the diarist Samuel Pepys (1633 – 1703) by James II, the chess board was handed down in the Pepys-Cockerell family.

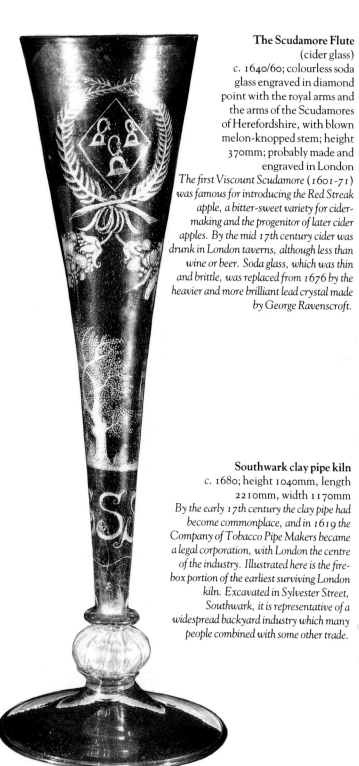

The Scudamore Flute
(cider glass)
c. 1640/60; colourless soda glass engraved in diamond point with the royal arms and the arms of the Scudamores of Herefordshire, with blown melon-knopped stem; height 370mm; probably made and engraved in London

The first Viscount Scudamore (1601-71) was famous for introducing the Red Streak apple, a bitter-sweet variety for cider-making and the progenitor of later cider apples. By the mid 17th century cider was drunk in London taverns, although less than wine or beer. Soda glass, which was thin and brittle, was replaced from 1676 by the heavier and more brilliant lead crystal made by George Ravenscroft.

Pair-case watch
1702; engraved 'LESTOVRGEON LONDON'; silver with mock pendulum movement in a pierced silver outer case; diameter of outer case 58mm

Many French and Dutch Protestant clock- and watchmakers settled in London during the 16th and 17th centuries. David Lestourgeon probably came from Rouen, and seems to have specialized in commemorative watches. This example records the death of William III.

Southwark clay pipe kiln
c. 1680; height 1040mm, length 2210mm, width 1170mm

By the early 17th century the clay pipe had become commonplace, and in 1619 the Company of Tobacco Pipe Makers became a legal corporation, with London the centre of the industry. Illustrated here is the fire-box portion of the earliest surviving London kiln. Excavated in Sylvester Street, Southwark, it is representative of a widespread backyard industry which many people combined with some other trade.

Sign from the Cock and Bottle tavern, at the
corner of Laurence Pountney Hill and Cannon
Street
c. 1700; delft tiles; 870 × 640mm
*The sign indicates that liquor was sold not only
from the cask but in bottles, i.e. to drink on the spot
or to take away. Taverns (for the sale of wine) and
ale houses proliferated in London streets, each
displaying its own sign.*

(Above right) **The South Sea Company Plate**
1715; silver-gilt; 279 × 178mm (cup and
cover), 101 × 356mm (salver on foot)
*Both the covered cup and the salver on its
detachable foot are engraved with the coat of arms
of the South Sea Company and were made in
London by Thomas Farren.*

John Dwight stoneware
c. 1675; red stoneware teapot fragment, bottle
with crowned letters CR, experimental
porcelain and sagger (fireproof clay case)
containing a misfired globular mug; excavated
on the site of Dwight's pottery
*John Dwight studied chemistry at Oxford and the
secrets of making German stoneware in
Lancashire. Although not the first English
stoneware potter, he set up kilns at Fulham in 1672
or 1673 and attempted to imitate Chinese porcelain
by making stoneware white and translucent.*

Modern London

The Museum's Modern Department deals with some two and a half centuries of London's most recent history, from 1720 to the present day. During most of that time the city lay at the heart of a great and expanding Empire and at the centre of a world-wide network of trade and commerce. It was in this period that London grew to become the world's first 'megalopolis', a vast concentration of people and buildings such as had never before been seen.

By the middle of the eighteenth century, London's crowded wharves and warehouses, great public buildings and newly constructed streets and squares already showed that it was a city of great wealth, political influence and creative achievement. London led the way in the manufacture of luxury goods such as silk, porcelain, clocks and watches and furniture, with which the increasingly affluent merchants and business classes decorated their homes. The Modern Department has built up collections which include not only the articles themselves but also the tools with which they were made and evidence of the workshops and the craftsmen who made them.

London in the eighteenth century was also a violent city, often erupting into riot and disorder. The volatile nature of the London crowd and the harsh treatment it received are reflected in the prints of Hogarth, in the poignant and dramatic evidence of carved inscriptions on the walls of prison cells, and in the formidable iron-clad door that once gave entrance to Newgate Prison. There are, however, many less sombre aspects of London in this period to be found in the appropriately-shaped rotunda of the Museum's eighteenth-century gallery which echoes that of one of London's most famous pleasure gardens, Ranelagh in Chelsea.

By the middle of the nineteenth century, when Britain was 'the Workshop of the World', London was its largest port and industrial centre, handling vast quantities of raw material and manufactured goods. London depended on overseas trade: even the mahogany counters and deal floorboards of the shops, such as can be seen in the Museum galleries, originally arrived by ship in the London docks. Thousands of men were employed in factories and in the Thames-side shipyards. Thousands more craftsmen were to be found all over the city in attic or backyard workshops attached to their homes. Since its inception, the Museum has collected a wide range of material, representative of more than forty London crafts and trades, dating back to the nineteenth century and earlier. Most of these items are at present in store, awaiting display at the proposed museum in Docklands.

The nineteenth-century gallery reflects the contrasts to be found in London during this period. While the Great Exhibition of 1851, held in the Crystal Palace in Hyde Park, proudly asserted the supremacy of British industry and manufactures, the coming of the industrial revolution and the rapid population expansion brought to London hitherto unprecedented problems of poverty, overcrowding and disease. To deal with these, services such as main drainage and new systems of urban administration had to be evolved. The Metropolitan Board of Works was founded in 1855, and its successor, the London County Council, in 1889. The 1870 Elementary Education Act laid the foundation of state education and was responsible for the appearance all over London of the Board School buildings that became a familiar feature in the London skyline. One display in the

Lifts from Selfridges
1920s; interior panels, 'Les Cigognes d'Alsace' ('The Storks of Alsace'), of wrought iron and bronze, by the French artist Edgar Brandt; exterior repoussé panels, painted bronze, depicting Zodiac figures, by C. A. Llewelyn Roberts; made by the Birmingham Guild Ltd

The building of the imposing entrance loggia of Selfridges store in 1928 completed its magnificent Oxford Street façade. The work of eminent decorative artists and sculptors was used as an integral part of the structure, to enhance the feeling of novelty, modernity and excitement in which all could share.

Museum includes features of the classroom that were once familiar to generations of schoolchildren.

The succession of transport revolutions that have succeeded each other during the modern period began with the introduction of the fast mail coaches, first introduced in 1784 on the London to Bristol route. They depended for their success on the improved turnpike roads, but were soon to be rendered obsolete by the railway that linked London with every part of the country. More crucial for the growth of the city was the development of a suburban railway network in the 1870s and 1880s and the subsequent extensive housing developments which enabled thousands of commuters to travel into London daily to work. In the present century, the motor car necessitated the provision of many miles of new roads, adding further to London's catchment area. While London led the world in developing a unified system of public transport, bringing together the underground and main-line railways, with a complex of bus services (featuring the famous red double-decker buses), it was, at the same time, becoming an international centre for air travel, with the building of Croydon airport (officially opened in 1928) and today's massive Heathrow, opened in 1948. All these changes affected the life and character as well as the size and shape of the city. The electronics revolution is now modifying London's forms and patterns of communication and employment, again altering its personality. These successive waves of innovation are reflected in the Museum's collections and displays, which include model mailcoaches, omnibuses and aeroplanes, and London Transport designs for everything from lighting to posters.

London has maintained an internationally acknowledged position in almost every form of entertainment. For centuries the theatre has played a central part in the social and creative life of London. At no time was this more so than during the nineteenth century. Apart from the great theatres in Central London, there were also dozens of 'minor theatres' (often, paradoxically, of great size) located in the densely populated inner suburbs, such as the Britannia Theatre, Hoxton, and the Surrey Theatre, Lambeth. The Museum's theatre collection is exceptionally wide-ranging, from costumes and models to playbills, tickets and programmes, theatrical portraits and 'Juvenile Drama' sheets.

Following the first public demonstrations in London of cinematography, in 1896, the 'flicks' quickly became popular, and film-making studios were established around London. During the next few decades these were to produce many famous films, for which London was often the setting. Besides housing material relating to film-making, the Museum also runs, in association with the National Film Archive, an extremely successful evening series of films, entitled 'Made in London'.

The most violent and tragic moment in the history of London in the modern period was the destruction of thousands of lives and buildings by bombing in the Second World War – a period recalled in a number of displays. The Festival of Britain in 1951 coincided with the post-war rebuilding programme which has so decisively changed the face of London.

London has always provided a point of entry to Britain for successive waves of immigrants, and one of the most notable changes since the war has been the arrival of many new Londoners, chiefly from those parts of the world that were once part of the British Empire. Their role in staffing the essential services of London and broadening the range of ethnic foods and restaurants available has been recorded by the Department. London is now, more than ever, a multi-racial community.

To attempt, as the Museum of London does, to hold 'the mirror up to nature . . . to show . . . the very age and body of the time', means something different to each department. To the staff of the Modern Department, it means collecting all kinds of evidence which not only reflects London's past but also the many changes that occur around us. Photography plays a vital role in recording these developments, as well as being of historic interest in itself. The Port of London Authority photographic archive in the Museum consists of some 20,000 images, spanning the years 1900 to 1965 and covering every aspect of the port, while more recently the staff of the Modern and Photographic Departments have recorded, for example, the demolition of Heston Airport and the last days of the original Billingsgate Market. Some of the Museum's photographs constitute the only surviving record of past features of London life.

Similarly, the Museum's considerable collection of printed ephemera, ranging from eighteenth-century trade cards to examples of modern packaging, preserves significant details of the passing scene. Printed material, banners, photographs and extensive archives relating to the women's suffrage movement are among the Museum's many well-known special collections.

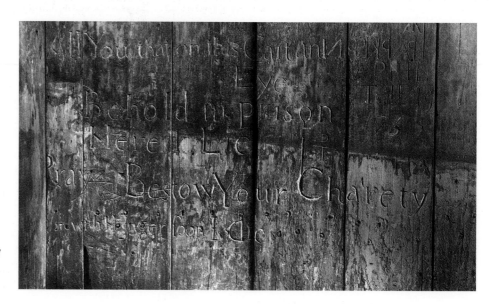

Ewer

1755-70; heavy lead glass, cut and polished;
2048 × 2000mm

*Large jugs such as this one feature on the trade
cards of fashionable London glassmakers, cutters
and sellers in the late 1750s and early 1760s.
Although glass objects rarely give any indication of
where they were made, 18th-century provincial
and American newspaper advertisements, trade
ledgers and London trade cards show that London
set the fashion for cut glass at this time. This jug
comes from the Garton Collection, of over 400
pieces acquired in the early 1930s. The recent
acquisition of the Whitefriars Archive, a collection
of papers and glass from the factory which, until
1923 was situated between Fleet Street and the
Thames, has enabled the Museum to begin working
on the London context for the fine glasses in its
collections.*

(Opposite) **Graffiti on a wall from Tower
Hamlets gaol**

Mid 18th century

*Tower Hamlets gaol in Wellclose Square was
typical of pre-Newgate prisons in London in that it
was not purpose built. Rooms were adapted for use
as prison cells simply by being reinforced, in this
case with oak planks and six-inch metal nails. The
graffiti reflect the amount of time that prisoners had
on their hands and also reveal that they were,
surprisingly, allowed to use sharp instruments. The
inscription reads: 'All you that on this Cast an Eye,
Behold in prison Here I lie. Pray Bestow Your
Charety, or with Hunger soon I die.'*

Pair-case watch
Hallmarked London 1786; gold and enamel
verge watch with gold, gilt and enamel
chatelaine *en suite*; diameter of outer case
45mm, length of chatelaine 105mm
*The verge movement is signed 'Tawney No. 1441
London' and the dustcover 'TAWNEY
Clerkenwell No. 1441'. The gold cases bear the
punch marks of the Clerkenwell watchcase-maker
Thomas Hardy. It is almost certain that the
enamelling was also done in the locality,
Clerkenwell having been for some time the
'quarter' for London's large number of watch- and
clockmakers.*

**(Opposite) Porcelain figure group: 'The
Dancing Lesson'**
c. 1762-69; Chelsea porcelain; marked with a
gold anchor; *c.* 410 × 350mm
*A couple sit beneath a flowered bocage
background, their clothes elaborately enamelled
and gilded, he playing a hurdy-gurdy while she
teaches a dog dressed in human clothes to dance.
This piece is an example of the finest, and last,
period of the Chelsea porcelain factory (the 'gold
anchor' period) in which the most elaborate and
highly decorated pieces were produced. The
porcelain tradition, stemming from the Continent
and ultimately the Far East, was introduced to
England via the important London factories at
Chelsea and Bow, and disseminated to the
provinces.*

Doll's house (the Blackett Baby House)
c. 1740; 1500 × 1220mm
*The Blackett Baby House (named after the family
for which it was made) is a typical example of the
superb quality of 18th-century dolls' houses, built
more as a miniature for adult pleasure than as a*
child's plaything. Each room provides a detailed
illustration of the organization and decor of a
wealthy household of the time, sometimes giving
evidence on furnishings and domestic equipment
known otherwise only from descriptions in the
literature of the day.

Trade card

1757; 270 × 210mm; engraver unknown
Trade cards were frequently used as both advertisement and bill, the account being written out on the reverse. In addition to providing us with valuable information about the clientele, the range of stock and current prices, the cards are often fine examples of the engraver's art.

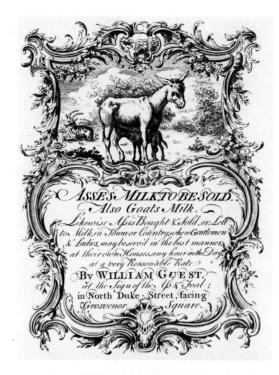

Commemorative pottery of the Great Exhibition

1851; diameter of plate 185mm, height of vases 220 and 167mm, average height of mugs 83mm
Six transfer-printed pieces of pottery, some monochrome, others coloured, all probably made in the Midlands. The popularity of commemorative pottery began in the 1780s with souvenirs of royalty, political struggles, famous heroes or great events, and reached its zenith with the flood of items for the Diamond Jubilee of Queen Victoria in 1897, when techniques for mass production and mass-produced surface decoration had become very sophisticated. The Great Exhibition, 'of the Works of All Nations', brought about largely through the enthusiasm of Prince Albert, was one of the outstanding success stories of the nineteenth century and resulted in innumerable types of souvenir, some of the most popular being in pottery. The subject of all of these pieces is the Crystal Palace erected in Hyde Park for the Exhibition.

Vale of Hornsey

(Above) *c.* 1855 by George Shadbolt; (right) 1982

In 1855 Hornsey was an area to the north of London characterized by open fields and quiet country lanes. Following the coming of the railways in the 1850s and 1860s, however, and with the shortage of space in central London causing people to move further out, Hornsey developed into a suburb. The old estates were broken up, speculative builders moved in, and by the end of the century the population of the parish, which had been only 7,000 in 1851, shot up to 72,000.

Theatrical portrait sheets
1812; published by William West; each c. 180 ×
230mm
*Printed sheets such as these were often available
within days of a new stage performance and are the
immediate precursors of the Juvenile Drama (or
Toy Theatre) sheets for young people, which
gained great popularity in the mid nineteenth
century. They come from the extensive Jonathan
King Collection, which was given to the London
Museum in 1911 and was thus among its earliest
acquisitions.*

Model of the Britannia Theatre, Hoxton
c. 1860, made by Peter Gorrie in 1975
*The often highly elaborate productions of
melodramas, ballets and pantomimes at the many
theatres in central and suburban London required
small armies of backstage technicians who were
employed to operate the trap doors and other
openings in the stage, raise or lower the painted
'flats' and backcloths and control the gas lighting.*

Dock cooperage
Late 19th century
The items in this reconstruction are among many thousands of objects recovered from London's docks, with the help of the Port of London Authority, in the early 1980s. Dock coopers were kept busy repairing barrels of port, sherry, rum, whisky, ginger, tobacco and other valuable imports, damaged in transit, and before distribution to merchants.

'A Convict's Home'
1877; photograph by John Thomson
A scene outside a cookshop in Drury Lane whose proprietor, a former policeman connected with the Royal Society for the Aid of Discharged Prisoners, extended a warm welcome and a helping hand to released convicts and 'ticket-of-leave' men. The photograph is one of thirty-seven which were taken by Thomson and published (by the Woodburytype process) in the book Street Life in London *(1877) with an accompanying text by Adolphe Smith. This is one of the earliest published works of social-realist documentary to make use of photography.*

Scale model of a late Victorian dustcart
c. 1895; wood and metal; 235 × 405 × 240mm
A rare surviving example of a manufacturer's working model, made by the firm of Constable and Son of Paddington Basin. It was estimated that the refuse of late-19th-century London included 1,000 tons of horse dung daily, constituting a significant health hazard. The introduction of refuse vehicles such as this helped to improve the health and well-being of Londoners.

Coconut fibre works, Millwall
1885; photographer unknown
Trade directories reveal that there were a number of these establishments in London during the latter part of the 19th century, where the coconut fibre was made into coarse mats and matting. As far as is known, no physical remains of the industry have survived, and this photograph is the only visual record which the Museum possesses.

Terminal buildings, Heston Airport
Built 1929, demolished 1978
Heston airport, near Hounslow, was an important
example of early airport design, but is now largely
forgotten. It was planned to cater for the
anticipated boom in private flying in the 1930s, and
was later adopted by British Airways. Prime
Minister Neville Chamberlain flew from here during
the negotiations with Germany in 1938.

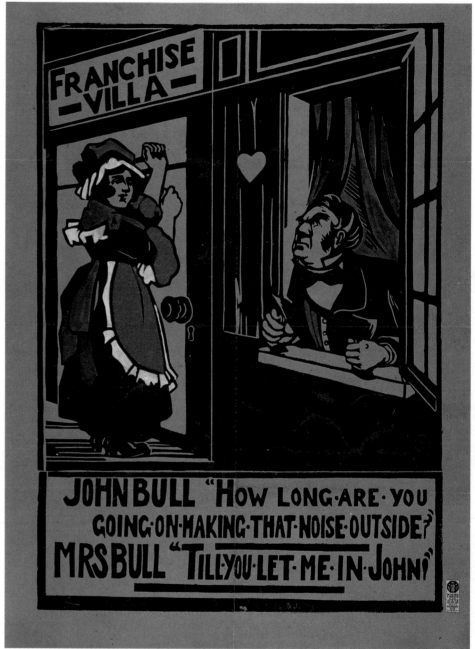

(Left) Schoolroom
c. 1880-90
The provision of education for all was one of the
major achievements of the Victorian age, and the
London School Board encouraged a wide
curriculum. Furniture and fittings were designed
with great care to ensure efficient control of large
classes.

Suffragette poster
c. 1913; published by Atelier; 760 × 1010mm
One of a range of posters designed and printed by
women at the 'Atelier', 65 Stanlake Villas,
Shepherd's Bush. It is part of a large collection of
items relating to the suffragette movement which
was donated to the London Museum in 1950 by the
Suffragette Fellowship.

Supermarket trolley
1978-84; chromium with red, plastic-covered
handle, child seat and rubber swivel wheels;
1160 × 800 × 560mm
*The supermarket trolley is illustrative of the trend
away from the local shop to the bulk-buying, fully
automated supermarket. The emphasis is on
efficiency and convenience, with the child seat
enabling customers to push both child and shopping
around the store with ease. 'Giant'-size packets
and a variety of foods, including health foods,
indicate 1980s fashions which may or may not
survive, while the packaging itself illustrates a range
of designs and materials currently in use. The
recording of present-day trends is a keynote in the
Modern Department's activities.*

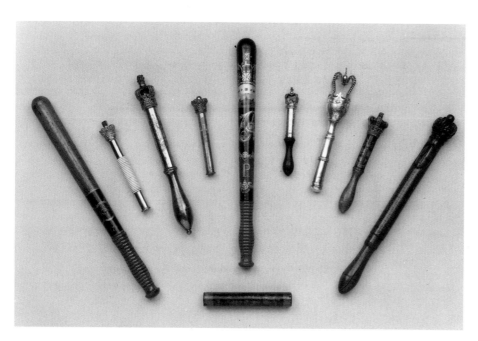

Tipstaves and constables' wooden truncheons
c. 1780-1880; silver; lengths 150-380mm
This group of truncheons and tipstaves is a sample of a large collection and illustrates the wide range of design and quality in objects once used for the enforcement of law and order. The tipstaves served as a type of 'identity card', demonstrating the authority of the bearer. Truncheons were usually painted by or for their owner, on his retirement.

Port of London Authority policemen
c. 1930
This photograph shows PLA police testing their life jackets at the West India Docks. All port employees were encouraged to learn to swim, and dock policemen were trained in life saving.

London film-making

1919-53; sound engineer's 'clapper' board,
illuminated indicator from Denham Studios
and painted sign from a door at Islington
Studios

*Of the many sites in and around London connected
with the fluctuating fortunes of the British film
industry, none are more famous than those of the
studios at Islington (opened in 1919, closed in
1949), associated particularly with the early
careers of producer Michael Balcon and director
Alfred Hitchcock, and at Denham (opened in
1936, closed in 1953, demolished in 1981), built
for the producer/director Alexander Korda.*

The Eagle Hotel and Garage, Holly Bush Hill, Snaresbrook

1931; photographer unknown
*This early example of a roadside inn and garage
provided facilities for the 'servicing' of both people
and their cars within easy motoring distance of
central London. Private motor vehicle ownership
rose steadily from the end of the First World War,
and by 1930 there were over 2 million vehicles on
British roads. At the same time the garage industry
developed, with the necessary mechanical expertise
provided by men who had received motor vehicle
maintenance training during the war. In the same
year that this photograph was taken, the Ford
Motor Company opened its factory at Dagenham
and so brought mass production to the car industry
in London.*

Costume and Textiles

The London Museum was one of the first museums to recognize the value of clothing as a social record. Clothing and textile items with a London relevance were collected assiduously from its inception in 1911, and today the Museum possesses one of the largest and most varied British costume collections, with a high international standing.

The earliest acquisitions came from archaeological sites, mainly in the City. As well as a very fine collection of footwear ranging from the time of the Roman settlement to the late sixteenth century, leather belts, parts of doublets and other accessories have survived in some quantities. Wet conditions have also enabled a large number of other items of Tudor clothing to survive: fragments of cloth, hose, caps, smocking, laces, cords, as well as a most interesting range of knitted items including caps, stockings, sleeves and a child's mitten and vest. The meticulous scientific techniques employed more recently in excavations have produced a very fine range of textiles, both silks and woollen cloths, representing imported and home-produced textiles of the tenth to the sixteenth centuries; of especial importance are a number of fragments which reveal the high quality of sewing techniques in the fourteenth century.

Until recently, high-quality fashionable dress was considered the only type of clothing worth collecting, and naturally predominates in the collection. For over seven hundred years, London has been an important centre of fashion and the clothing industry, as a result of the presence of the monarch and Court, as well as of a rich and expanding merchant class. The collection is fortunate enough to have an impressive range of both male and female clothing of the seventeenth, eighteenth and nineteenth centuries. There was much less competition in acquiring such objects earlier in the century, and consequently it was possible for the Museum to obtain some outstanding examples of seventeenth-century clothing as well as an enviable range of eighteenth- and nineteenth-century dresses and suits. Sadly, fashionable clothing of the twentieth century was not collected until after the last war; nevertheless a good representative range has been assembled and is frequently augmented.

Because of its broad social outlook, the Museum has also attracted a wide range of clothing other than fashionable wear. Simple everyday and working clothes have not been collected until fairly recently, and are therefore not so well represented for earlier centuries, but many occupations are still today instantly recognizable through special clothing (traffic wardens or public transport staff, Santa Claus or Wimbledon ball boys, for instance), and it is vital that clothes such as these are preserved for the future.

The Museum has an exceptionally large and varied collection of civil and ceremonial uniforms. The Church, the Law and the City are well represented, while the presence of the monarch and court in London has helped to create an impressive array of colourful court and ceremonial dress, including robes of the various royal orders. Such peculiarly London clothing as that of the Yeomen of the Guard, Thames Watermen and 'Pearlies' also has a place in the collection.

Supplementing the clothing is an extensive collection of accessories of all types and all dates for men and women; infants' and children's clothing is also acquired, though there are gaps, inevitably, in the earlier periods. There is a limited range of flat textiles and embroideries which represent typical artefacts of their time or, more importantly, the products of local industries. Here the co-operation of colleagues in the Modern Department is essential, so that the working conditions and tools of the clothing and accessory industries are properly recorded. Fashion plates and photographs, instruction manuals and trade catalogues are all vital adjuncts to a collection of clothing.

Coronation dresses and robes
1937; London
These dresses were worn by Queen Elizabeth the Queen Mother and her daughters Princess Elizabeth and Princess Margaret at George VI's Coronation on 12 May 1937. The gold embroidery on the dress and purple State robe of the Queen Mother incorporates flowers representing the British Isles, the Dominions and the Empire. The Princesses' dresses are of white cotton Leavers lace, and their purple velvet robes are decorated with bands of gold lace.

In view of the importance of the clothing industry in London, the Museum has made especial efforts to represent the major branches of the industry, from production to retail. Originally, London was the home of many important industries – tapestry weaving, silk and cotton weaving and printing, for example – a fact now often forgotten, and so besides the textiles themselves, the Museum also possesses artefacts connected with their manufacture, such as silk and braid looms, warping machines and printing blocks. A similar approach is taken to the industrial manufacture of clothing, and to distribution through wholesale and retail outlets. In areas like this there is close co-operation with the Modern Department, and photography is seen as a valuable recording tool, supplementing what can only ever be a minimal assemblage of objects.

Also housed within the Costume Department is the Museum's large collection of dolls which covers the period from the late seventeenth century to the present day and includes many fine examples of wood, wax and ceramic: these are part of the Museum's larger collection of children's toys. Wax doll-making was an especially important small industry in London and embraced such famous names of the doll world as the Pierrotti family and Mme Augusta Montanari. Included in this collection is the unique group of over one hundred tiny wooden dolls dressed by Queen Victoria when a young girl.

The Museum is without doubt most famous for its extensive collection of English royal clothing. This was initiated as the result of George V's involvement in the foundation of the London Museum at Kensington Palace, when a group of coronation robes were lent. The lively interest shown in the Museum by Queen Alexandra and Queen Mary brought much more royal material on permanent loan or as gifts, and the popularity of these in displays has, in turn, attracted more material. The collection now extends back as far as the childhood boots of Charles I as well as the knitted vest he is believed to have worn on the scaffold in 1649. Not surprisingly, the majority of the royal personalia comes from the nineteenth and early twentieth centuries: an interesting group of items once the property of Princess Charlotte of Wales (1796-1817), a great many items spanning the whole of Queen Victoria's lifetime and those of all her children, and a smaller assemblage of clothing and other accessories previously the property of her grandchildren and great grandchildren.

Before the advent of the Theatre Museum, the London Museum was the principal repository for theatre-related material and, therefore, an imposing collection of theatrical costume has been developed. Its main strength is a large group of costumes worn in London productions by Britain's first theatrical knight, Sir Henry Irving (1838-1905), and by such colleagues and contemporaries as Ellen Terry, Sir John Martin-Harvey, Gordon Craig and Constance and Frank Benson. Other aspects of the performer's art are also covered – clowning, opera, ballet and music hall – and costumes from television and more recent stage productions have extended the way in which the world of entertainment in London is represented.

The size and range of the Museum's costume collection is now such that it cannot adequately be shown in the main display galleries nor in occasional special small exhibitions. The construction of adjacent display facilities is now being considered and a 'Friends' organization was set up in 1980 to aid with fund raising. It has been most successful in attracting interest to the collection, channelling help to the department and organizing a regular programme of lectures and other events.

Tudor knitwear
Probably mid 16th century; London
Knitted items of clothing rarely appear in contemporary paintings, and little information can be gleaned from documentary sources. Therefore the finds made in the City earlier this century, mainly to the north-west, are of considerable importance since they record many details about the techniques, wools and dyes employed in their making. Caps of all sizes and shapes form the majority of the finds, followed by socks and stockings, and women's sleeves; the child's vest and mitten illustrated here are unique, the latter of particular interest because of the decorative band knitted in a contrasting colour. These, along with the remnants of cloth and leather clothing, are poignant reminders of the working and business community of the City, many of whom could not aspire to the rich clothing of the nobility.

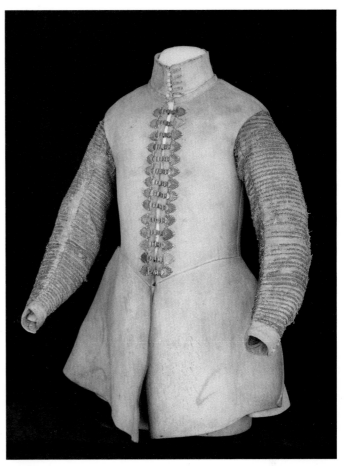

Dress

1720–30; English

Of a fine pale yellow silk, this open robe is the earliest dress in the collection. It has the wide, weighted sleeves typical of the early 18th century, and the presence of unpicked stitching indicates that it may have been modelled from an earlier dress. The elaborately arranged skirt, pinned or buttoned back, is of a type found occasionally throughout the first half of the 18th century. The quilted petticoat is of a slightly darker silk and probably did not originally belong with the dress.

Buff coat

1620–30

This coat, made of buff (thick, oil-tanned oxhide), is fastened with decorative metal hooks and eyes. The sleeves are of a finer, more supple skin ornamented with bands of narrow silver braid. Highly practical for military wear, buff came into fashionable use during the Civil War, and this coat is a fine example of the marriage of practicality and fashion. The Museum has several examples of this type of garment.

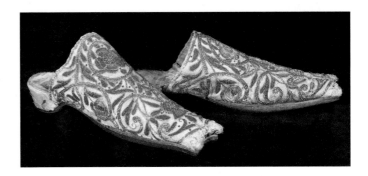

Men's mules

1660–80

These long narrow shoes, intended for informal wear, are of red satin embroidered with a design incorporating roses and thistles in laid coiled gold and silver thread. It is fortunate that material of this high quality was collected early in the London Museum's history, for little now survives and the Museum is rarely able to acquire early material.

Full dress suit

1775 – 80; possibly French

The coat, of cut and uncut black velvet figured with coloured silks, is heavily ornamented with embroidery in coloured silks, mainly in satin stitch. It is further enriched with spangles and coloured glass paillons, similar decoration being applied to the cream satin waistcoat. The breeches do not match the coat and, though contemporary, are probably a later replacement. Such rich formal wear was usual for ceremonial occasions and is well represented in the Museum's collection.

Shirt and breeches

1600-50

This outfit lacks any documentation, but is believed to have been worn by a sailor. The shirt is of embossed linen, the breeches of twilled cotton and linen with a turned bone button at the front waistband fastening. Sailors' clothing was distinctive from early times, since conditions on board ship required practical, flexible attire which would withstand rough wear and yet dry easily. Working clothes or 'slops' such as these were made by riverside tailors in areas like Billingsgate and were sold ready-made from an early date. It is exceptional for working clothes of any period to survive.

Dress

1883 – 86; made in London by Halling, Pierce and Stone

This dress is a typical example of the high class dressmaking industry of London. It is of deep blue silk satin trimmed with matching satin figured with coloured flower sprays, and gold satin; an ornamental blue bead trimming encircles the neck and cuffs. The makers, at Waterloo House, Pall Mall East and Cockspur Street, had been in business as early as 1817 as linen drapers. In 1886 they were amalgamated with Swan and Edgar Ltd, a merger typical of the way in which old-established London firms helped to form the large wholesale and retail empires of the twentieth century.

(Right) Stage costume of Anna Pavlova

1909–11; Russian; designer unknown

When the ballerina Anna Pavlova died in 1931, her husband, M. Victor Dandré, decided that the London Museum was the most appropriate home for her remaining costumes and other personalia. Of these, the costume for 'The Dying Swan' is the most famous, but the dress for 'Russian Dance' best portrays the ballerina's origins. It is of cream silk lavishly ornamented with red silk, gold braid and imitation jewels. The costume is known to have been worn in 1909, and was shortened in 1911.

(Below) Stage costume of Edmund Kean

c. 1830

Worn by Edmund Kean (1787–1833) as Richard III, probably his most famous Shakespearean role and the one in which he made his last appearance at Drury Lane in 1833. The doublet, baldric (red sword-belt) and trunk-hose are of black cotton velvet ornamented with spangles, pastes and imitation ermine. The crowned helmet is of pasteboard adorned with large pastes and imitation ermine. The costume was given to the Museum by the Thorndike family and is one of its earliest theatrical costumes.

(Right) **Wedding dress of Princess Charlotte of Wales**
1816; made by Mrs Triaud of Bond Street
*The dress is of white silk machine net richly embroidered
with silver strip, with a formal court train and
underskirt of silver tissue. It was worn by
Princess Charlotte of Wales (1796–1817),
the only child of George IV and Princess Caroline
of Brunswick, when she married Prince Leopold
of Saxe-Coburg-Saalfeld in the Great Crimson
Room at Carlton House on 2 May 1816.
This was the last occasion on which an English
royal bride wore the traditional rich metallic
tissue appropriate to her rank; soon
afterwards royal brides adopted the
fashionable all-white wedding dresses,
although some silver was still often
incorporated into their dresses.
They continued to wear court
trains.*

Wax doll
1870–80; London
*A doll made to be dressed as a child but here wearing the long
embroidered robe of a baby, together with appropriate underwear.
This doll was made in the cast wax technique by Charles Marsh of
London and was sold by E. Moody in the Soho Bazaar, on the
north side of Soho Square. Such dolls were sold dressed in
elaborate contemporary fashions, but could also be purchased
undressed; it is likely that this one wears homemade clothing.*

Court dress

1922; designed by Lucile, London

This dress was worn by the donor at her first Court presentation in 1922. It is of pale pink silk satin trimmed with beads and imitation pearls; the court train is of pale pink georgette and cream silk Spanish lace trimmed with silver braid. 'Lucile' was the trade name of Lady Lucy Duff Gordon, and her couture house, then at 23 Hanover Square, was the first of international importance to make London its main base. The Museum has a small collection of the designs which she circulated to her clients.

Stage suit

1972–73

This one-piece stage suit is of black elasticated satin ornamented with serrated bands of black suede pierced with silver eyelets, worn with black leather gloves. It belonged to the pop star Alvin Stardust, and epitomizes the era of carefully devised image-making in the mass entertainment industry. Alvin Stardust was born in Muswell Hill and enjoyed a first career as Shane Fenton before adopting a new name and image.

Pearly King's suit

Late 19th century; made in London

Although the Pearly tradition is now so closely associated with London, it is in fact barely a century old. It originated in the 1880s when London costermongers (sellers of produce from barrows) *began to ornament clothes with pearl buttons for fund-raising events. The suit of 'F. Bliss, Pearly King of Islington', is one of the earliest to have survived. Employing an already well-worn suit of heavy dark blue cloth, the owner has decorated it with buttons in typical Pearly motifs –* horses' heads and shoes, fish, anchors, playing cards, plants in pots, roses, clowns and butterflies – *which refer to various aspects of the costers' lives. On many later Pearly outfits the button decoration takes over, covering the whole ground and destroying what is often witty visual symbolism.*

The unique character of London has been recorded by artists since the sixteenth century, as the Museum's collection of over 20,000 paintings, prints and drawings bears ample testimony. The collection was formed for historical purposes rather than aesthetic considerations – to provide visual evidence of the development of London and the lives of its inhabitants. Although it does not contain any paintings by the major artists who revolutionized the image of the capital – Hogarth, Constable, Turner or Monet – it does include a number of works of outstanding importance, besides many others well-loved by generations of visitors to the Museum and made familiar through reproduction. Furthermore, it provides an essential source for students of almost every aspect of London's history over the last four hundred years.

The Museum possesses the earliest painted view of London from a distance, which dates from the 1620s. The artist, who was probably Flemish, depicted the city and the Thames from above Greenwich, surrounded by fields and hedgerows. More detailed seventeenth-century topographical paintings are rare, but the collection includes the earliest known view of Chiswick, executed in the 1670s by Jacob Knyff.

Of exceptional rarity are the paintings recording and commemorating major events in the history of seventeenth-century London. The depiction of Charles II's state entry into London in 1661 by Dirck Stoop, the earliest known painting of a royal entry, is a spectacular record of the lavish procession deliberately staged to blot out memories of London's mixed loyalties during the Civil War. The most important surviving representation of the Great Fire of 1666 hangs on display nearby. Thereafter, the lives and pleasures of

Londoners were recorded with increasing frequency, and the Museum possesses two paintings of Londoners disporting themselves on the frozen Thames by the Dutch artist Abraham Hondius, who settled in England in 1674.

Prints of individual London citizens were published by Wenceslaus Hollar in the 1640s, but it was only with Marcellus Lauron that the comparatively realistic representation of street sellers – as opposed to early generalized woodcut series – was introduced to England. The Museum possesses a set of his engravings, *The Cryes of the City of London*, first issued in 1687, bound in a single volume, as well as the major eighteenth-century series of street cries. Furthermore, a collection of the beautiful original drawings for Paul Sandby's *Cries of London* (1760) was acquired in 1965 and there are several Rowlandson watercolours, showing his noticeably more cynical interpretation of the subject.

The eighteenth century witnessed an enormous growth in the market for topographical prints, which celebrated the construction of new streets and squares, public buildings and private mansions, bridges and monuments in the expanding capital. The collection contains most of the major published series and also the original watercolours for a number of them by artists like Joseph Farington and Thomas Malton II, as well as by their early-nineteenth-century successors, R.B. Schnebbelie and the Shepherd family. The most prominent eighteenth-century paintings include one of Canaletto's rare interior subjects, Henry VII's Chapel in Westminster Abbey, an unfinished but impressive view by Samuel Scott of Covent Garden Piazza, and three important works by William Marlow, notably his serene prospect

DUTCH SCHOOL
The Fire of London
1666; oil on canvas; 897 × 1516mm
The artist evidently knew London well and was probably an eye-witness to the Fire. It is seen from a boat near Tower Wharf. The great exodus from the City is set within the three main landmarks of medieval London, the Tower, London Bridge and the glowing shell of Old St Paul's, beneath a night sky alive with sparks.

of the London river-front from Westminster to the Adelphi theatre, painted in the early 1770s.

The Museum's collection of works by Thomas Rowlandson deserves special mention. It includes three major watercolours dating from the 1780s, generally considered to be the artist's finest period: *Skaters on the Serpentine, Taking Chocolate at the White Conduit House* and *Showing Off in Rotten Row*. There are, in addition, studies of genteel soirées and promenades, City merchants and chop houses, semi-rural tea gardens, views of the river between Woolwich and Richmond, depictions of burly tradesmen and lascivious servants, all drawn in his inimitable style with panache and humour.

The technological achievements of Victorian London are symbolized by the Great Exhibition of 1851, whose crowded halls are recorded in the famous chromolithographs on display, while the dramatic glass palace in Hyde Park is seen from beyond the Serpentine in a painting by Thomas Dibdin of the opening of the exhibition. One of the most famous paintings in the collection presents another aspect of the changing city: John O'Connor's painting of St Pancras Hotel and Station from Pentonville Road at sunset. Viewed from the rise to Islington, the neo-Gothic spires of Sir Gilbert Scott's St Pancras Hotel and the huge vault of the station itself attain a mythic scale.

In contrast, the Victorian predilection for genre painting introduced many more down-to-earth representations of urban life into the artist's repertoire. Charles Hunt's depiction of a coffee stall and John Henry Henshall's watercolour, *Behind the Bar*, line up carefully chosen cross-sections of Londoners, providing enough visual clues for us to be able to unravel their identity and relationship with one another. A softer and more decorative interpretation of everyday life is provided by two of the Museum's most popular paintings: John Ritchie's *A Summer Day in Hyde Park* and *The Bayswater Omnibus* by George William Joy.

At the same time, many amateur artists were recording London with a sense of identification and accuracy of detail rarely found at more elevated artistic levels. Robert Allen, for example, painted the delightful oil of his tobacconist's shop off Grosvenor Square. The collection is rich in such valuable documents, not only of buildings long demolished but also of trades whose practices have changed out of all recognition.

The representation of twentieth-century works of art is growing in strength. The first professional artists wholeheartedly to identify with London for their *raison d'être* were members of the Camden Town Group before the First World War. The collection includes one of Sickert's music-hall oil studies, characteristic paintings by Robert Bevan and Charles Ginner, two paintings by Spencer Gore in contrasting Impressionist and Post-Impressionist styles and a number of works on paper by these artists. Aspects of Christopher Richard Wynne Nevinson's art can be studied in a group of his paintings in the collection, ranging from a late Futurist interpretation of Fleet Street and St Paul's, *Amongst the Nerves of the World,* to Impressionist views of the river. In recent years the Museum has also purchased a number of important studies by other major artists not usually associated with the depiction of London: David Jones's watercolour of St John's Wood and Eric Gill's prospect of Lots Road Power Station, for example.

The Museum received a group of works from the War Artists' Advisory Committee in 1947, including memorable images of the London Blitz by Henry Moore, Graham Sutherland and John Piper. Over the last thirty years, because of the dominance of abstract techniques and the enormous growth in documentary photography, comparatively few artists have used London as a source of inspiration. Yet significant acquisitions have been made. A group of works by Ceri Richards includes not only drawings of traditional costermongers but also light-hearted depictions of Trafalgar Square which encapsulate the spirit of the Festival of Britain. The continuing cycle of urban demolition and renewal is recorded in the powerful expressionist drawings of Leon Kossoff. It is hoped that the growing emphasis on draughtsmanship and the return to more representational styles will encourage new generations of artists to depict not only features that are about to be lost, but also the vital present of this great metropolis.

WENCESLAUS HOLLAR (1607-77)
Summer
1644; etching; 258 × 180mm
This print, one of a set of the Four Seasons, was executed during Hollar's first period in England, when he was in the service of the Earl of Arundel from 1636 to 1644. It successfully combines Hollar's interest in costume and topography, the fashionably dressed lady being placed against a background of St James's Park, with the Banqueting House and Old St Paul's in the distance.

THOMAS ROWLANDSON (1756-1827)
Taking Chocolate at the White Conduit House
1787; pen, watercolour, pencil; 257 × 365mm

The White Conduit House, Islington, was a tea garden converted from a tavern in the early 18th century. Customers here gather round an organ.

PAUL SANDBY (1730-1809)
Mop Sellers

1759; pen and watercolour; 193 × 151mm
One of 12 watercolours by Paul Sandby of Cries of London owned by the Museum. These, and 64 others in a similar style, were executed in 1759 with the idea of making prints after them. Only 12 etchings, however, were published, in the following year. Sandby's gallery of London characters is the most important series of Cries between Marcellus Lauron's influential set dating from 1687 and the better-known groups executed by Francis Wheatley and Thomas Rowlandson in the 1790s.

ABRAHAM HONDIUS (c. 1625-91)
The Frozen Thames, Looking Eastwards towards Old London Bridge

1677; oil on canvas; 1078 × 1756mm
This is the earliest known painting of the frozen Thames. The arches of Old London Bridge reduced the tidal flow of the Thames to about a quarter of today's speed, and until the bridge's demolition in 1828 the river would freeze periodically. The freeze depicted here is that of December 1676 which began to break early in January 1677, and the state of the ice is represented with great accuracy.

Roderigo (Dirck) Stoop (c. 1614-83)
Charles II's Coronation Procession
1662; oil on canvas; 640 × 1990mm
*The coronation procession through London
originated with Richard II in 1377 and ended with
James II in 1685. Charles II's cavalcade through
the city took place on 22 April 1661, the day before
his coronation, and is recorded by the artist with
great attention to detail. The procession winds
through four specially erected triumphal arches,
which commemorate Rebellion vanquished by
Monarchy, London's maritime prosperity, the
Temple of Concord and, as the King leaves the
city, the Garden of Plenty.*

Canaletto (Giovanni Antonio Canal)
(1697 – 1768)
**Interior of Henry VII's Chapel, Westminster
Abbey**
c. 1750; oil on canvas; 650 × 577.5mm
*Canaletto arrived in London in May 1746 and
stayed for nearly ten years, returning to Venice
only for short intervals. He found many influential
patrons and depicted their properties, but most of
his English views were of London and its environs.
This canvas shows one of his rare interior subjects –
others being King's College Chapel, Cambridge,
and the Rotunda at Ranelagh. The view is taken
looking eastwards, with the tomb of Henry VII in
the centre.*

GEORGE WILLIAM JOY (1844-1925)
The Bayswater Omnibus
1895; oil on canvas; 1206 × 1725mm
*The characters in this particularly appealing example of
Victorian genre painting are described by the artist as follows:
'In the farthest corner sits a poor anxious mother of children,
her foot propped on an untidy bundle; beside her, full of kindly
thoughts about her, sits a fashionable young woman; next to
her the City man, absorbed in his paper; whilst a little milliner,
band-box in hand, presses past the blue-eyed, wholesome
looking nurse in the doorway.'*

HENRY MOORE (b. 1898)
Women in a Shelter
1941; watercolour and oil crayon; 480 × 423mm
*Henry Moore was commissioned to make a series of drawings
of London underground subjects between 1941 and 1942.
His response reflects the impact of war but also relates to his
monumental figure studies of the 1930s.*

J.A.M. WHISTLER (1834–1903)
Rotherhithe
1860; etching and drypoint, 3rd state; 270 ×
197mm (plate mark)
*In 1859, Whistler took lodgings in London's
docklands and began a series of ten plates of the
Thames.* Rotherhithe, *the only print dating from
1860, looks across the Thames to Wapping and
north-west to the dome of St Paul's in the distance.*

ROBERT ALLEN (dates unknown)
Allen's Tobacconist Shop
1841; oil on canvas; 578 × 502mm
*This charming view of the exterior of The
Woodman, a tobacconist's shop at 20 Hart
Street, Grosvenor Square, was painted by the
proprietor, Robert Allen. As advertised outside,
Allen was also a sign painter. The posters on the
left advertise plays such as* Highlife below Stairs,
Twenty Years of a Guileless Life *and
Shakespeare's* As You Like It, *as well as trips to
Dover and Margate.*

(Left) John Henry Henshall (1856-1928)

Behind the Bar

1882; watercolour; 402 × 720mm
This interior of a typical public house in late Victorian London is reminiscent in its subject matter of Edouard Manet's famous Bar at the Folies-Bergère, *also painted in 1882. Henshall is, however, mainly concerned with narrative detail.*

(Above) Eric Gill (1882 – 1940)

Lots Road Power Station

1911; pen and ink and watercolour; 127 × 215mm
The building of Lots Road power station began in 1902, to a design by the American engineer James Russell Chapman. Consciously American in style and size, it was constructed to supply electricity to the underground. This bold yet atmospheric study seems to affirm Gill's belief that engineering was 'often work of extraordinary beauty in the living sense that beauty is power made visible'.

Robert Bevan (1865 – 1925)

A Street Scene in Belsize Park

1917; oil on canvas; 750 × 903mm
This view shows the junction of Buckland Crescent (left) and Belsize Park, near the artist's home. The large house in the centre was acquired by the Hall School in 1916 and is still used as a preparatory school.

David Bomberg (1890 – 1957)
Evening in the City of London
1944; oil on canvas; 698 × 908mm
Painted from the tower of St Mary-le-Bow looking west, the view sweeps round from a gleam of river on the south (left) over the familiar profile of St Paul's to Cheapside on the north (right). The gaunt outlines of London buildings after the blitz provided Bomberg with fitting subject matter to explore his fundamental concern with underlying forms. However, in this work (the only oil Bomberg executed of London during the Second World War) the drawing is enhanced by richly orchestrated textures to create a harmonious tonal scheme. It is an optimistic image, expressive of a firm intent to survive. As such it is among the most important icons created of London during the last war. The painting was bought in 1985 with help from the National Heritage Memorial Fund and the Museums and Galleries Commission Purchase Grant Fund.